CHRISTCHURCH THEN & NOW

IN COLOUR

JOHN NEEDHAM

The History Press

First published in 2013

The History Press
The Mill, Brimscombe Port
Stroud, Gloucestershire, GL5 2QG
www.thehistorypress.co.uk

ISBN 978 0 7524 7156 3

Typesetting and origination by The History Press
Printed in India.

CONTENTS

ACKNOWLEDGEMENTS

I would like to take this opportunity to thank my parents for giving me permission to use many of the old photographs of our family within this book. Researching this book took me on a personal journey. I spoke to my parents, who showed me some old photographs of Christchurch and of my family's connections in the area. For example, Bosley Farm Tea Gardens was run by my great-grandmother, and at one time my great-great-uncle used to run the Blackwater Ferry; my grandfather used to own and run St Catherine's Dairy, which my parents inherited and ran until it was taken over by Unigate in the late 1960s.

I would also like to thank my wife Chrys for reading and correcting the text within the book. Many thanks also to Sue Newman for spending the time to look over and check many of the historical entries within the book, and Alex McKinstry, who kindly let me have some historical information on Christchurch.

ABOUT THE AUTHOR

John Needham has lived in Dorset all of his life. Over the years he has worked for Plessey's/Siemens; in Southampton on gas turbines; and in London for Tate & Lyle, which included travelling the world inspecting sugar refineries; and then on to the gas and oil industry.

A dedicated collector of archive images of the county, John devotes his spare time to writing local history books, which he finds very rewarding.

INTRODUCTION

Christchurch, population of 47,300 and sited between the rivers Stour and Avon, is dominated by the great Priory, which for hundreds of years could be seen from any point within the town. The original site proposed for the Priory was to be on St Catherine's Hill. Legend has it that each time building materials were taken up the hill they would be spirited back down the hill, to the site of the present church, the following night. In the end the builders of the church constructed the church on the present site. The original Saxon church did not survive: in 1094 it was demolished and the building of the Priory was started by Ranulf Flambard (later to be the Bishop of Durham). The building was completed in 1150. The Priory escaped the destruction of the monasteries by Henry VIII in 1539, but when he gave the Priory to the parish the monks left and the monastery was pulled down. The Priory gave the name to the town: Cris-Churche de Tyenham, which eventually became Cristes-Chirche.

Over the years Christchurch has seen many changes, and today it contains many historical features: the castle and Constable's House, for example, both now just ruins. They were demolished during the Civil War when the town was captured by Lord Goring. Bridge Street contains the oldest council house in England, now a perfumery. Next door, on the left-hand side of the building, was the site of the old court house. When the court house became old and dilapidated it was demolished and a back room in what is now the perfumery was used for a few years in its place.

In the eighteenth and nineteenth centuries the town saw its fair share of smuggling: John Streeter and Slipper Rogers operated within the area, landing great cargoes of contraband at the Haven or along the coast at Hengistbury Head and outwitting the revenue officers. The most famous incident involving smuggling is probably the Battle of Mudeford in 1784, when revenue man William Allen was killed.

Christchurch was also famous for the manufacture of fusee watch chains. Robert Cox began manufacturing such chains in 1790 in a factory in the High Street, and by 1793 he had gained the monopoly for the manufacture of chains and employed forty or fifty children. The average wage at that time was 6s or 7s a week. In 1845 William Hart opened a similar factory in Bargates: this stayed open until the late 1890s, when it was sold. In Quay Road, which runs next to the Priory, you can find the Red House Museum, once the town's workhouse.

Christchurch was also an important trading port, and the harbour was a shelter and safe mooring for many a traveller. The fishing fleet would sail from the harbour, fishing for turbot, soles, whiting, mullet, herring, mackerel or salmon. Then, during the summer months, they would catch shrimps and prawns.

Over the years Christchurch has flourished, and it has much to offer the many visitors that flock to the town each year.

ST CATHERINE'S HILL

A VIEW LOOKING across Hurn Road from St Catherine's Way during a 1950s winter. At this point in time St Catherine's Hill had not yet been developed. The name 'St Catherine's Hill' comes from a chapel that once stood on the hill. The hill covers around 35 hectares and rises to a height of 45m. There is a fantastic view from the top. However, the steep sides have protected the hill from the advances of time and the developers. The hill has been occupied for centuries: there are eleven tumuli or barrows surrounding the ridge of the hill. Bronze-Age and Iron-Age settlers may have built enclosures just to the south of the radio mast. The hill has been used through the years as a military training centre, as a base for the Royal Horse Artillery from Christchurch Barracks,

and by soldiers from both world wars (who used the hill for trench-war field training and as a grenade-throwing range).

St Catherine's Hill was supposedly the original site for the Priory. The Priory was eventually built on the flood plains between the Rivers Stour and Avon.

A VIEW FROM the same point today, looking across Hurn Road and up Marlow Drive. The first records I can find of Marlow Drive are from around 1967. The parade of shops appears for the first time in *Kelly's Directory* in 1969. The Catherine Wheel pub has long gone, replaced by a block of flats and community centre. The shops have changed hands many times through the years, apart from one: Lambe the butcher's. Today St Catherine's Hill is managed by Christchurch Borough Council's Countryside Services and ARC (Amphibian & Reptile Conservation Trust) along with the Friends of St Catherine's Hill, a group that was formed in 2008. The tree cover over the hill has increased from 25 per cent to 75 per cent, as can be seen from the photographs in this book.

GROVE LANE

VIEW DOWN GROVE Lane from the junction at Fairmile Road. This was taken in the late 1920s/ early 1930s when, as you can see, it was still a narrow country lane. Grove Lane formed part of the Jumper's Common and originally was part of Hurn Parish. To the left could be found the 100ft fir tree which became a local landmark. It was approximately 200 years old and part of an ancient forest. Sadly, however, the tree was damaged in 1954 and had to be removed (as the

next page shows). In 1936 the Grove was widened by about 16ft. This brought the house and bungalows closer to the road edge, as can be seen in the modern photograph.

THE SAME VIEW in January 2012: this is now a very busy road linking Fairmile Road, Jumper's Corner, Barrack Road and Iford. The road has been widened and a roundabout added at the junction to Fairmile Road, but if you look carefully you can see that the line of oak trees are still there – although some have died and been replaced. Others have been lost due to alterations in the road layout or for safety reasons, as happened at the junction to Bosley Way where the trees were removed.

THE GROVE TREE

THE REMOVAL OF a landmark at the top of the Grove in the 1950s was met with great opposition, but went ahead nonetheless. Part of the cause was doubtless the need to widen the junction: as you can see, the road is already wider than that which can be seen in the 1930s image on the previous page, and it is wider again in the modern image. A crowd has gathered around the tree, and a policeman can be seen directing the traffic – and possibly also the spectators who have gathered to watch the tree come down.

THE JUNCTION OF the Grove and Fairmile Road. A roundabout has now been added to help with the increase in the volume of traffic using the junction.

OAK AVENUE

TWO VIEWS DOWN Oak Avenue and the Grove, one with the shops on your right and one looking towards Iford. These photographs were taken in around the 1920s when, like many parts of Christchurch, the area was just a winding country lane. The Grove Farm Estate had been broken up at this time. Alexander J. Abbott & Son's estate agents looked after the sale of Grove Farm Estate and produced a set of plans showing the farm divided up into plots. The Grove Farm Estate may have had a connection with the Priory before the Reformation: one barn on the site was built on the site of a demolished Roman Catholic church; legend has it that there may have been an underground tunnel from the church which led to the Priory at Christchurch.

The River Stour skirts along the edge of the estate for half a mile. Part of the proposal demanded that a strip of land be reserved for riverside walks, and several areas were to be set aside for playing grounds, bathing spots and cricket fields. A further 2 acres of land adjoining the river and farmhouse was reserved for lawn tennis and other recreations.

A VIEW DOWN Oak Avenue in January 2012, which is now totally unrecognisable as the area seen the earlier photograph. In the inter-war period, suburban housing estates started to take over from farm and woodland. However, if you travel down Hurn Way until you reach Stour Way you will

find a small wooded area; this provides a glimpse of what the area must have looked like before the onslaught of developers. The shops are still here today: although they have changed hands many times, they still serve the local community.

BOSLEY WAY

THIS PHOTOGRAPH SHOWS what Bosley Way looked like in the early 1930s, not long after the break up the Grove Farm Estate. I know this property well, as I was brought up here. St Catherine's Dairy was behind the property for many years, and I can remember as a child the milk floats going off early in the morning to deliver the milk. The property then was resting on a large piece of land approximately 50ft wide and 300ft long, in gardens (unlike today).

In the seventeenth century there was a large common associated with Bosley, defined by the parish boundary on the east side of the River Stour, River Way on the west side and the line of Old Barn Road on the south side (which extended up onto St Catherine's Hill).

BOSLEY WAY IN 2012. The area then was totally different: the surroundings have now been totally developed, and bungalows have been built on the land behind my parents' house.

BOSLEY FARM
TEA GARDENS

BOSLEY FARM TEA Gardens. These pictures show the Tea Gardens between 1908 and 1912.
The picture below shows the cottage and surrounding area; the one below right shows
my great-grandmother, Eliza Hayward, and great-grandfather, Robert Hayward, with my
grandmother Gertrude Louisa. The building was a two-up, two-down cob-walled thatched cottage
from around the seventeenth century. By the twentieth century the farm had been reduced to a
fraction of its size. My grandmother was born at the farm in 1888. The cottage stood in around
40 acres. They kept pigs and cows, and to help with the income they also ran the Tea Gardens. The
charabancs made their way from Bournemouth, going down the rough track (now St Catherine's
Way) to the Tea Gardens. They would stop for Sunday afternoon tea at the establishment before
heading back to Bournemouth. In 1920, Lord Malmesbury sold the cottage for the sum of £1,100
to F.W. Welch. However, it carried on as a tea garden.

THE COTTAGE IS still here today but it is no longer on its own – it is now surrounded by bungalows and newly built houses. The present owner inherited the property from his father who had purchased the property in 1955 with the intention of turning it into a pub. The area has been built up and the cottage now finds itself closed in.

Evidence of a Saxon settlement within the area has been found: when an extension was built onto the cottage in the 1980s, sherds of pottery were uncovered dating from between the ninth and fourteenth centuries – and even more were found in the back garden.

IFORD VILLAGE

THIS POSTCARD CONTAINS a view of Iford village, looking up Water Lane, in 1905. The view shows an idyllic village scene with thatched, mud-walled cottages and typical country gardens. Iford became well known as a safe fording place to cross the river: with its eyelets, or small islands, it was easily fordable on horseback. In the dry season you may even have been able to wade across the river. This practice carried on until the first bridge was built across the River Stour.

Iford's crossing was used by the smugglers of the seventeenth and eighteenth centuries, and there is a story about one of the smuggler's

helpers; in 1762 William Manuel was suspected of informing on the smugglers, and had a visit one night from one such group. They dragged his son, Joseph Manuel, out of the house and across the moors to Decoy Pond House at Bournemouth. There he was forced onto a smugglers' vessel and taken to Alderney – where, by a miracle, he managed to escape, although he was badly injured in the attempt.

IFORD VILLAGE TODAY. The area has undergone many changes, not least with the demolition of the cottages. Directly in front is a children's nursery built in the late 1920s as a sports/community hall for the local residents of Iford and just out of the picture, to your left, is a very good little tea house. Here you can sit outside and take in the beautiful views across the river. Today the area is frequented not by smugglers trying to cross the river but by tourists and locals coming down to the river to walk their dogs, or – as I have done – to feed the ducks from the old bridge across the river.

IFORD ROUNDABOUT

A 1950S VIEW across the junction of Castle Lane and Barrack Road, with Castle Parade to the left of the picture, built on the grounds of Iford House (built in 1795 and demolished in 1936). The area marks the boundary between Christchurch and Bournemouth. Notice the latticework of cables for the trolley buses heading off to Christchurch (or turning left and heading off down Castle Lane). The trolley buses first ran into Christchurch from 1936 and continued to run until 20 April 1969, when they were taken over by diesel buses.

If you travelled down Castle Lane in years gone by and followed the river you would have found a small natural valley which slopes down to the river. Here you would have

discovered a small concrete jetty which went out into the river, just below the water level. This spot was locally known as 'sheep wash' – and, as the name suggests, was where the locals would bring their sheep to be washed before they were sheared. Up to 500 sheep would be washed here. Many shearers would travel around the area in the season, charging 4*d* per sheep.

TODAY WE SEE a very different view. The overhead cables were removed with the demise of the trolley buses. At the centre of the junction we now see a highly decorated and very busy roundabout. The parade of shops is still there, and the Iford Bridge Tavern can still be found on the opposite side of the road and out of view. The river has had its course altered and the sheep wash is no longer there.

ST CATHERINE'S DAIRY

ST CATHERINE'S DAIRY, and my grandfather out delivering milk. This image was captured in around the early 1930s. Notice that there are no milk bottles – only a cart which he pushed from door to door and a churn of milk from which he would measure out a pint or half pint into a jug – and no such items as cream, which then was a luxury. At the time, St Catherine's was a local dairy and, as such, it only served the local community. It could only cover as wide an area as he could walk! This picture was taken in Hurn Way, which is a short distance away from the dairy in Bosley Way.

THE SAME VIEWPOINT today. You can just make out the gateway to the bungalow, which must have been well made as it is still there. The view has changed slightly these days: Springfield Road has now been built, and the hedges and trees have also matured.

BLACKWATER FERRY

BLACKWATER FERRY IS sited not far from where the Spur Road
now runs. It was at this point that you would have been able to cross
the River Stour. The ferry was only a short walk from Christchurch
(approximately 3 miles) or from Holdenhurst village. The walk
from Christchurch to the ferry would have taken you through the
rhododendron forest, which in May would have been a mass of different
colours. As you came out of the forest you would have been met by a
view across the river of fertile green meadows. I have been told that one
of my distant relatives used to be the ferryman who helped people across
the river. These images show Hurn Road and the ferry in the early
nineteenth century. As you can see, the crossing was made on a punt
and cable – you can just make out the cable. The River Stour, unlike
the River Avon, flows slowly and placidly throughout its course until it
reaches the sea, making the crossing of the river an easy prospect.

THE AREA IS now totally unrecognisable; the house and crossing have
long gone, to make way for the widening and building of the main road.
The main Hurn Road is now a very busy road linking Christchurch
with the airport.

VIEW FROM ST CATHERINE'S HILL

A VIEW FROM St Catherine's Hill in the late 1920s. This photograph was taken during the break up of Grove Farm Estate. The picture shows Hurn Road, with Hurn Way running off at right angles. Hurn Road runs along the spine of the ridge between the River Stour and the River Avon.

Off Hurn Way can be seen Bosley Way and on the left of the picture a few houses can just be made out: these would be on Grove Lane, in those days just a country lane. Going down towards Hurn and the area known as Bosley Farm you would come across a track which, if you followed it, would have taken you down to the Bosley Farm Tea Gardens. The track today is followed by St Catherine's Way at the bottom of Marlow Drive.

THE SAME VIEW in January 2012, taken from what I believe to be the same spot. The trees have taken over, and you can no longer see down from the hill. The whole area has been fully developed. A number of extra developments have also taken place where the back gardens of the houses have been in-filled with expensive bungalows or houses.

BARRACK ROAD

A VIEW DOWN Barrack Road, at the junction of Beaulieu Road, in May 1929. It was named after the barracks that could be found further up Barrack Road towards the town. Barrack Road also used to be the direct route from Bargates down to the river crossing on the River Stour at Iford. The post office can be seen on the corner of Beaulieu Road. This is a much more rural

view of Christchurch, with a car driving down what looks like a dirt track, passing a horse-drawn cart. The car is passing by Jumper's Corner, named after the Jumper family who owned the estate. To the left of the picture the Gospel Hall (also known as the tin church, due to the building materials used in its construction) can just be made out.

THE SAME VIEW in March 2012: once more the progress of time has changed the view, although some of the houses on the left are still standing. The large white house to the right of the picture can be seen in the earlier photograph. The old post office is now a KFC. The road has been widened, making the front gardens smaller, to accommodate the volume of traffic which now travels down the Barrack Road en route to Bournemouth and surrounding areas.

BEAULIEU ROAD

A VIEW DOWN Beaulieu Road, Stourvale, in the early part of the twentieth century. Note the horse-drawn vehicle coming down the unmade road. I would say that these were fairly new buildings at the time this postcard was created. The area on which Beaulieu Road is built on was

locally known as Bernards or Burnetts Mead. Several roads in the area reflect this: Burnett Road and Avenue, and Bernards Close. At No. 3 Beaulieu Road lived Mrs Smith, a flower seller who would travel into Bournemouth every day and set up a pitch outside Beales. This carried on until 1943, when Beales was bombed. After this time she had a pitch in Bournemouth Square.

THE SAME VIEW today – and what a difference! This is now a one-way street lined with cars, a slightly less sedate view of one of our local roads. It now opens up onto one of the busiest roads in Christchurch, Barrack Road, with the local KFC on the corner, once the local post office.

VIEW FROM TUCKTON BRIDGE

VIEW FROM TUCKTON Bridge in the 1930s. Just in view is the tower of the Priory: at this time the Priory could be seen from nearly anywhere in the town.

There are several boatyards located within the town, one being Elkins' Boatyard, located on the River Avon. In 1934 they built three river boats for the owners of Tuckton Tea Gardens, the Christchurch boating enthusiasts Messrs Newlyn and Ball, for the ferry service from Tuckton Tea Gardens: the *Headland Queen*, *Headland Belle* and the *Headland Pal*. In 1935 the *Headland Maid* was added to the fleet. They would ply their trade from Tuckton Tea Gardens, stopping off at Wick Ferry, Christchurch Quay, before heading off to Mudeford. All the vessels were specially designed to suit the harbour conditions: of a shallow draft, fully loaded the vessels would only draw 18in of water.

In 1920 a flying boat arrived here. It landed in the harbour to deliver an urgent dispatch to a number of VIPs within the area, causing great excitement.

THE SAME VIEW in January 2012: a slightly more developed river bank than in the 1930s. The houses along the river bank all have moorings and there are a few more pleasure crafts moored along the river today – but alas, the new developments obscure the view of the Priory. The four ferry boats built by Elkins' boatyard are still working today. The only time they stopped working the route was during the war, when the vessels were taken over by the navy. They returned to service after the war. The service starts each year at Easter and finishes around the end of October, running most days (weather permitting). The harbour itself is subject to double high tides, resulting in long periods of high water level – great for the sailors and yacht enthusiasts! For years the local sailing groups have enjoyed this fact; I've spent many happy days myself sailing around the harbour.

TUCKTON BRIDGE

TUCKTON BRIDGE, BUILT in 1905 by Yorks Hennebique Ltd of Leeds. The bridge is 360ft long and 29ft 6in wide. Built of reinforced concrete, it rests on fifty ferro-concrete piles. The longest span of the bridge is 41ft (at the centre), and the remaining spans are only 25ft 6in. To mark its opening on 17 October 1905, the first tram between Bournemouth and Christchurch crossed the bridge. To use the bridge you would then have had to pay a toll: this system stayed in place until 1943. A four-wheeled vehicle cost 6*d*; a pedestrian was charged 1*d* to cross the bridge. The bridge was originally built to carry twin tramways

across the River Stour and was one of the first substantial reinforced concrete bridges within the UK and one of the earliest in Europe.

TUCKTON BRIDGE ON a warm winter's day in January 2012. The bridge carries the B3059 across the River Stour and also marks the boundary between Christchurch and Bournemouth borough. This photograph has been taken from the opposite bank of the River Stour due to the advance of time and the construction of houses, all with moorings for the boats and pleasure vessels that now use the river. Access to the bank is now gone. In 1997 the bridge was given a weight limit of 13 tons. It is one of the main routes from Bournemouth to Christchurch, and the bridge has been a busy route for over 100 years. In 2012 the bridge underwent extensive repairs to sections of the concrete structure, to improve the drainage, kerbing and road surface (which was replaced). The bridge was closed for a short time, though one of the pedestrian paths was left open to allow the public to cross the river. Historically no two trams were allowed to cross each other on the bridge and this carries on today with the buses that cross the bridge.

TUCKTON CREEKS

TUCKTON CREEKS IN 1912, looking down the River Stour, with the Priory in the distance. Notice the couple in the picture: maybe they are off for a trip on the river on a sunny Sunday afternoon?

Before becoming Tuckton Tea Gardens, the establishment here was known as Tuckton Creeks. It was a boating business and a tea rooms combined, with light refreshments offered to visitors. The property was leased and owned by a Captain William Maxwell Brander. The captain was one of Southbourne's earliest inhabitants, living in Twynham Road in a house called 'Spiekers', built in 1871. In 1904 he moved to West Close at Wick. Brander's Lane is named after him.

The building in the picture, the pavilion, was given planning permission in 1905. Before that, teas were served on the deck of a lugger which was beached within the basin. Then, in 1919/1920, the lease passed on to two Christchurch boating enthusiasts, Messrs Newlyn and Ball. This is when the tea rooms were renamed Tuckton Tea Gardens. These carried on as two businesses: the husbands ran the boating side, and the wives ran the tea gardens, the latter running until the late 1940s. During the 1950s the business was run down until, in 1964, Bournemouth Corporation purchased the freehold.

TUCKTON CREEKS IN January 2012. This photograph had to be taken from a slightly different viewpoint. The whole area has changed and developed, mainly with the tourist in mind. Just around the corner can be found a café, and if you carry on walking along the river bank you will pass the Wick Ferry. Carry on again and you will find yourself at Hengistbury Head.

THE PRIORY

A VIEW OF the Priory, looking across the River Stour, at the turn of the twentieth century, with what looks like a canoe floating in the river. The Priory is a magnificent structure standing at the south-west of the town and on rising ground between the two rivers, the Stour and the Avon. The tower rises to a height of 36.5m and, as such, is visible from most corners of the town. Standing on the top of the tower is the salmon weather vane, a symbol of Christianity. In the tower is a belfry containing thirteen bells (an upper and a lower peal). Two of the bells date from 1370. Christians have worshipped on this site since the seventh century. The present building was constructed in 1094 by Ranulf Flambard (later Bishop of Durham), and the main church was completed in 1150. In 1539 the Priory escaped the wholesale destruction associated with the Dissolution of

the Monasteries. However, Henry VIII seized the monastery and all of its properties and gave them to the town; then the monks had to leave. The last prior at the Priory was John Draper, 'a very honest and conformable person'. John Draper was allowed to leave the Priory with a pension of £133 6s 8d, and lived – until his death in 1552 – at Somerford Grange. His grave was discovered near the quire screen in the nave in 1811. Eventually, in 1822, his tombstone was moved and preserved. It can be found in front of the chantry door built for him in 1529.

A SIMILAR VIEW in January 2012. This is not from exactly the same spot as the original, but this does show how tranquil the river bank can be on a warm winter's day. Even today the Priory looks over Christchurch, although, due to development, you can no longer see the Priory fully.

WICK FERRY

WICK FERRY AROUND 1911. Here the boat is loaded with people, all ready to cross the River Stour – maybe for a day out in Christchurch? Wick Ferry was started in around 1815 to provide employment for a farmhand called Marshall who had been injured and could no longer work on the farm. The ferry was then passed on to his son-in-law, Mr James Miller, who in turn left the ferry in his will, dated 1876, to his son, Eli. Eli was later to leave all his worldly possessions, including the ferry, to his widow, in October 1884. She ran the ferry until 1903, when it was put up for sale by auction. The sale of the business was not an easy one as the ownership of the ferry was questioned: who really owned the title, and was the river in fact a right of way? The report on the sale of the business in the *Christchurch Times* (27 June 1903) took a clear position, however: 'the

franchise was the property of Mrs Miller and no one can say it is not'. Combined with the ferry was also a boating business which comprised of thirty-eight boats, punts and the ferry boats. Mr J.C.E Edmunds of Wick Lane purchased the business and ran the ferry until 1946, when he retired.

THE VIEW ACROSS the river is very different today. Not such a grand staging point for the ferry: the shelter has long gone, and you are taken over the River Stour in a less sedate manner. The ferry runs every day, weather permitting, from Easter right up to the end of October, and from 10 a.m. to 5 p.m. During the winter the ferry also runs on a Saturday, Sunday and Monday, from 10 a.m. to 4 p.m. If you see the flag flying on the pontoon then the ferry is running.

CHRISTCHURCH ARMY CAMP

AN ARMY CAMP in Christchurch, Dorset. I believe this is of a First World War camp on Grove Farm Meadow, as during that conflict there were many army camps around Christchurch. I have investigated the picture and believe it may be an army canteen. However, if you look to the back of the photograph you can just make out sides of meat, so perhaps they are making soup? If anybody knows anything more about this photograph, or about the camp, I would be most interested to hear from you.

GROVE FARM MEADOWS in January 2012, the flood plain for the River Stour. Today it is used by local football teams, and locals walk their dogs on it. To the rear of the photograph is the River Stour, and to the right of the picture can be found Grove Farm Holiday Park. Iford golf course can be found just around the corner from the Meadows.

CHRISTCHURCH
RAILWAY STATION

CHRISTCHURCH RAILWAY STATION in 1908. The railway came to the area in 1847. At that time the trains only stopped at Holmsley: to get to Christchurch, you would have had to catch the horse-drawn omnibus. In 1862 the trains finally reached Christchurch via a branch line from Ringwood, and by 1883 Christchurch joined the main line, making the town more accessible to visitors and tourists. The branch line between Ringwood and Christchurch closed in the early 1930s.

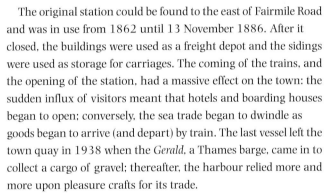

The original station could be found to the east of Fairmile Road and was in use from 1862 until 13 November 1886. After it closed, the buildings were used as a freight depot and the sidings were used as storage for carriages. The coming of the trains, and the opening of the station, had a massive effect on the town: the sudden influx of visitors meant that hotels and boarding houses began to open; conversely, the sea trade began to dwindle as goods began to arrive (and depart) by train. The last vessel left the town quay in 1938 when the *Gerald*, a Thames barge, came in to collect a cargo of gravel; thereafter, the harbour relied more and more upon pleasure crafts for its trade.

CHRISTCHURCH RAILWAY STATION in January 2012. The Christchurch line is on the South-Western main line, and from here you can travel to London Waterloo or down to Weymouth. Not much has changed here since 1908, save that the track is now fully electrified and has a third rail. In 2012, the station celebrated its 150th anniversary. The Christchurch Railway Station Friends gathered here, along with the mayor, Cllr Peter Hall, and dancers, music and song. The train station is quite long and can accommodate up to eight carriages – longer trains only use the first five carriages.

CHRISTCHURCH HIGH STREET

LOOKING SOUTH DOWN Christchurch High Street towards Church Street in 1905. This view cannot have been created long after the trams started running through Christchurch. The No. 31 is going to Poole, sharing the road with horse-drawn vehicles. On the left of the picture can be seen the Town Hall, originally built in the Market Place in 1745. However, this building was dismantled in 1859 and then rebuilt using some of the same materials. This reconstruction began

the following year. Standing behind the Town Hall in 1902 was a technical school. To the right of the picture is the home of James Druitt, town clerk and one of Christchurch's well-known inhabitants, built in the 1840s. The house was ultimately left to the county council in February 1947 and now houses the town's library.

THE SAME VIEW in early January 2012, with the Christmas decorations still up. The Town Hall and the area have changed. The hall behind the Town Hall, which became part of the council buildings, was demolished in 1979 when the council moved to Bridge Street. The Town Hall was then restored. The Mayor's Parlour is on the first floor; the ground floor was left open, as shelter for the market traders, when the rebuild went ahead in 1983. This was when the Saxon Square shopping area was opened. Looking down the High Street, one can see many of the same buildings. Behind what is now Toni & Guy can be seen the spire from the Elim Pentecostal church in Millhams Street.

CHRISTCHURCH HIGH STREET, LOOKING NORTH

A VIEW LOOKING north down Christchurch High Street; this photograph was taken at the time of the funeral procession for the late King Edward VII. As you look down to the end of the High Street you can just make out the Antelope Hotel, one of the many pubs in the town. In front of

the Antelope Hotel was one of the town's many landmarks, the fountain. The Town Hall is to the right of the picture. Pound Lane (where any stray animals, including cattle, were taken and could be found by their owners) came out next to the pub.

THE SAME VIEW in January 2012: free of crowds, but notice how the area has changed. The same fountain can be seen today at the junction of Bargates and the Fountain Roundabout. At the end of the High Street today, where once stood the Antelope Hotel, now stands a large roundabout which takes you on to the Christchurch bypass or down Bargates or Barrack Road. The Antelope Hotel, along with many of the shops going down Barrack Road, was demolished in the late 1950s to make way for the new bypass. Some buildings, however, can still be recognised. On the left of the picture can be found the old Fountain Hotel, which is today a shop.

CHURCH STREET

AN EARLY VIEW down Church Street. This postcard shows how the Priory dominates the view. As there are no tramlines in this photograph, we can conclude that it must have been taken before 1905 – around about the turn of the twentieth century. Notice the horse-drawn vehicles, the sign of a less hurried life. In the distance can just be made out the Eight Bells, a famous smugglers' drinking den. Sadly, however, this is no longer an inn: it served its last pint in 1907 and today it is a gift shop.

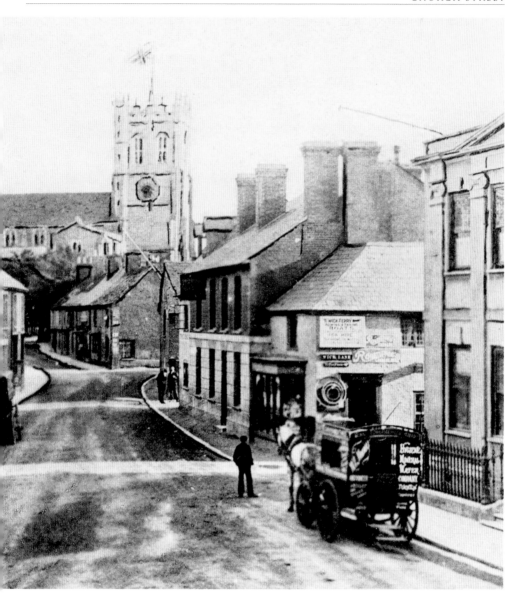

THE SAME VIEW in January 2012. As you can see, much has changed: great swathes of Church Street have been redeveloped. However, many of the buildings on the left of Church Street have survived the ravages of time and the developers. Within the courtyard of the building on the right, the old trolleybus turntable can still be found.

THE VIEW
FROM THE TOWER

A VIEW DOWN Church Street from the Priory tower. You can just make out Ye Olde George Inn on the corner of Castle Street, the light refreshments and tea shop nearby and the spire of the Congregational church in Millhams Street (now Elim Pentecostal church).

Right in the centre of the picture is the Dolphin Inn; the tram depot was here, and the trolleybus turntable can still be found in the car park at the Dolphin Centre. If you look carefully down Church Street you can see that the overhead tramlines are not yet in place: this would indicate that this view was captured before 1905. The original Dolphin Inn was destroyed in December 1864 by fire, only to be rebuilt in the following years. The building was demolished in 1973 to make way for shops and offices. Then, further down Church Street, can be seen another famous inn, the Eight Bells – a smugglers' haunt. On one occasion, the revenue men came to search the inn before the landlord had had time to hide the last keg. However, a quick-witted woman noticed the keg and sat down on it. She shook out her long skirt, covering the keg, and then proceeded to bathe her baby. The revenue men allowed her to carry on, and nothing was found. Legend has it that there is a tunnel from the Eight Bells which runs out to the Ship in Distress at Stanpit.

THE SAME VIEW today. Ye Olde George Inn is still there, though the tea rooms are now a shop. In the background is St Catherine's Hill. Many of the old features of the town remain, but many more have been lost forever.

YE OLDE GEORGE INN

YE OLDE GEORGE INN, now a Grade II listed building. It was originally known as the George and Dragon, but due to confusion with the brewery it was renamed. It was once an old coaching inn and a stopover for the Emerald Coach which travelled between Lymington and Poole. A tram is coming down the High Street, which would make this view more recent than 1905.

TODAY WE FIND a similar view down the High Street, with the inn to the right. Inside the inn, within the courtyard, you'll find a plaque that tells

the story of the George. There are tales of tunnels under the inn built to allow smugglers to make a hasty retreat from revenue men such as Abram Pike, but so far no tunnels have been found. The old timber-framed building was refaced in the eighteenth century with brick. Coming down the High Street we see a modern diesel bus – maybe running the same route as the tram once followed?

NORMAN TOWER AT CHRISTCHURCH PRIORY

THIS POSTCARD SHOWS the Norman tower at Christchurch Priory in 1905. There are indications, though no records, to show that at one point there may well have been a central tower over the crossing. It may well have collapsed, damaging the Norman quire; perhaps this was why

it was replaced with the great quire that stands today. A new tower was erected at the west end of the church in the fifteenth century. It is 36.5m tall. On the top of the tower is the salmon weathervane, a symbol of Christianity and also a reminder of a local tradition: the first salmon of the season is always presented to the prior.

A SIMILAR VIEW of the Norman tower at Christchurch Priory in January 2012. The tower today contains thirteen bells, which provide an upper and lower peal. Two of the bells within the tower date back to 1370.

THE AVENUE AND
NORTH PORCH

A VIEW FROM 1939 looking down the avenue of Dutch elm trees towards the North Porch. The North Porch was used in the early days as a meeting place for the 'Sixteen', the burgesses who met before the times of the Town Council. The North Porch was also used for weddings, as the church did not want its celibate monks to be involved in wedding ceremonies.

THE SAME VIEW in January 2012. The view has radically changed: the avenue of trees succumbed to Dutch elm disease and had to be removed. However, as you walk through the main gates from Church Street you now have an unhindered view of the Priory in all its splendour. Some famous visitors have walked the avenue of elm trees: Kaiser Bill, Queen Victoria's grandson, and the last German emperor strolled here in 1907 during his visit to the town.

PRIORY MILL AND QUAY

A VIEW OF the mill around the turn of the twentieth century showing a section of the quay where the fishermen would draw up with their boats and unload their daily catch. Place Mill dates back to Anglo-Saxon times, and the site is mentioned in the Domesday Book as part of the property of the canons of the Priory; it was then worth 30*d*. The mill escaped the Dissolution of the Monasteries of 1539, and was in use – and ground corn – up to 1908, when it closed. The building was used for

a number of years as a boat house. Place Mill is run by the mill stream, which is fed from the River Avon and then joins up with the River Stour in the harbour, linking the two rivers.

THE MILL IS now a Grade II listed building. In 1981 the mill was fully restored by the borough council and was reopened as a craft centre. During the summer months the mill is used as an art gallery, allowing local artists to display their work. The milling machinery is still in place and gives the visitor an idea of what the mill must have been like when the building was fully operational. Within the mill is also a display of milling artefacts. Entrance to the art exhibition is free and it is well worth a visit.

CONVENT WALK

CONVENT WALK IN the 1920s. It was opened to the public in 1911 to commemorate the coronation of King George V. The walk runs from Place Mill by the quay and follows the mill stream down to the bridge. It crosses over the stream at Mews Bridge or Millhams Bridge. On the left of this picture you can see the ruins of the Constable's House, and in the centre you can see a building still known today as Quartley's (after the surgeon who lived there). There is a story attached to

this man: one evening, he was called to attend upon a smuggler who had been shot. His reward – or payment – was a barrel of brandy which he found on his doorstep early one morning.

When the bridge over the River Avon was extended the building to the right of Quartley's was demolished.

CONVENT WALK IN 2012. As you can see, the trees have grown to such an extent that you can hardly recognise the scene. This is a peaceful walk, either into Christchurch or down to the quay.

CHRISTCHURCH HARBOUR

I UNDERSTAND THIS view is from the Christchurch Quay looking out to the harbour in the 1930s.
It looks like a father is watching on whilst his son plays in the harbour. The harbour and quay
has been the lifeline of Christchurch and has seen many changes. In 1653, a new entrance into
the harbour was cut, though it was damaged in 1730. Then, in 1762, when the government was
looking for another deep-water port on the South Coast for the navy, John Smeaton (famous as the
builder of the Eddystone lighthouse) was tasked with seeing how the harbour could be improved.

In 1771 the canal builder Brindley carried out a survey on the River Avon, and in 1836 J. Sylvester put plans forward to dredge the harbour to allow coasters to dock at the quay. However, in 1837 the plans were modified to allow the harbour to be used by pleasure crafts, as it is today.

Records left by Abram Pike, the local customs man, shows how Christchurch was to rely on the sea for the everyday commodities used by the local community: tea, vinegar, tallow and candles, to name a few. Christchurch also had a very good local industry and commodities used to leave Christchurch by sea; beer, for example, on route to Portsmouth.

A VIEW LOOKING out to the harbour in January 2012. I am not positive that this is taken from the same spot, but it may well be – I took this from behind Christchurch Sailing Club within the new housing development. If you look to your right, you can see the River Avon is joining Christchurch Harbour. In the distance, the Isle of Wight can just be made out.

THE CONSTABLE'S HOUSE

THE CONSTABLE'S HOUSE in July 1910. This Norman building was built by Baldwin de Redvers (the 2nd Earl of Devon) in around 1160 within the original castle bailey, with walls up to 9ft thick. At the time it was a place of luxury. The storehouse was downstairs; the main hall was upstairs,

reached by both an internal stairway and an external stairway. The hall contained a fireplace with a cylindrical chimney and was for the use of the resident constable of the castle. The view in 1910 shows the building overrun by ivy – not much of the brickwork is visible.

THE IVY WAS removed in the 1950s, after the building was donated to the town by Charlotte Druitt, revealing the building in all its glory and showing some fantastic features such as the cylindrical chimney, one of only five examples in the country. If you look to the centre of the picture you will see a structure hanging over the mill stream: this was the privy. Now a Grade I listed building, it will be protected for all time.

THE PRIORY AND RUINS OF THE CONSTABLE'S HOUSE

A VIEW ACROSS the River Avon of the Priory and the ruins in around 1903, taken before the Convent Walk was opened in 1911. The Constable's House next to the Priory still has ivy growing over it. The Priory was built in 1094 and escaped the worst ravages of the Dissolution of the Monasteries by Henry VIII in 1539, the year in which Henry gave the Priory to the town. However, the monks still had to leave the monastery, and the monastery was afterwards demolished.

TODAY THE PRIORY is virtually out of view as the trees and bushes have now matured, but the view really has not changed much for hundreds of years: the River Avon still flows out into Christchurch Harbour, meeting up with the River Stour and the mill stream flowing down to drive the milling wheel in Place Mill.

BOWLING GREEN AND
THE KINGS HOTEL

AN AERIAL VIEW of the bowling green and the King's Arms Hotel (now the Kings), both along Castle Street. The Christchurch Bowling Club, which dates back to 1925, uses the King's Arms bowling green, located opposite the King's Arms and next to the Constable's House in Castle Street. As you can see in the photograph, there is a game in full flow: I wonder who is winning?

THIS PHOTOGRAPH WAS taken from the Priory tower on a sunny winter's day. Though you can see the bowling green and the Constable's House, the Kings Hotel is just out of shot to the left. However, as you can see, very little has changed through the years. The Christchurch Bowling Club still use the green today. You can see many of Christchurch's famous features here too, including Dr Quartley's house and the River Avon.

TOWN BRIDGE

A VIEW OF Town Bridge in
1923 – or Quartley's Bridge,
as it came to be known. As
mentioned earlier, the bridge
was named after Dr Quartley,
whose house was on the narrow
strip of land between the Little
Avon and the mill stream. The
bridge was widened in 1899 to
allow for more traffic. Before the
Christchurch bypass was opened
in 1958 this was the main
route through the town and on
towards Highcliff and the forest.

VIEW OF THE bridge on a sunny winter's day in 2011. The view has not changed in the intervening years: the trees and shrubs have matured, but that is about it. Note the fishing boat in the river. I can remember seeing in the summer fishermen casting their rods, hopeful of catching a fish or two.

The bridge is made up of five low arches. If you look between the arches you can see cut waters and a parapet above. In days gone by, only small, low vessels could pass through the arches – any sailing vessels would have broken their masts whilst passing under the bridge.

THE NEW FOREST PERFUMERY AND TEA HOUSE

THE NEW FOREST Perfumery and Tea House is the oldest building within Christchurch other than the Priory. Built over 700 years ago, it still stands in Castle Street next to the castle gateway. The original courthouse, where the courts leet were held, was to the left of the perfumery until it was dismantled in 1884; the back room of the perfumery was used for court business and the election of the mayor and burgesses. Evidence of the sentences of the court of old can be found close by – such as the set of replica stocks and, across the road, the ducking stool in Ducking Stool Lane. When you visit the tea rooms you can find evidence of its previous use as a butcher's shop: if you look out the front you can see the meat-hanging

rails above the ground-floor windows, and in the back parlour you can find hooks in the beams where the meat would have once hung.

THE NEW FOREST Perfumery and Tea House on a winter's day in 2011. This establishment is a regular winner of the *Daily Echo*'s Best of the Best Tea Rooms in Christchurch, so not only is it a place where you can get one of the best cups of tea around but also a place where you can see thirty fragrances, all blended and bottled on the premises. It is now a Grade II listed building, and perhaps the oldest council house in England. Records show that it was a private house until the fifteenth century, when it passed to the council. The medieval timber-framed construction has been changed through the years: for example, the infill between the timber frame is now red brick where originally it would have been wattle and daub.

PLACE MILL BRIDGE

A VIEW OF Place Mill Bridge, a medieval bridge which crosses the mill stream. The oldest parts of the bridge, the arches, date back to Saxon times. The bridge is also known as 'Canon's Bridge'. Old Place Mill is in the background. Place Mill was, at one time, one of the monastic buildings belonging to the Priory. Place Mill and Canon's Bridge are important parts of the town's history and as such are Grade II listed structures. The mill stream itself was widened by 10ft in 1837 at the expense of Sir George Tapps-Gervis.

PLACE MILL BRIDGE in 2012. To the left is the Christchurch Yacht Club. The area has been developed over the years, making this a busy area with some exclusive and expensive properties. If you cross the bridge from the Priory and turn left following the mill stream, you will be walking along the 'Converts Walk' which will take you down to the Town Bridge and past the ruins of the Constable's House.

BARGATES

A VIEW DOWN Bargates in 1919. This looks like an army procession. Not long after the war, on 19 July 1919, the streets of Christchurch were decorated with banners and flags to celebrate the end of the war and the return of British troops from the various fronts. A large crowd gathered to greet the local men and there was an air of celebration and of great relief that the war was over. A large bonfire was lit in the evening on Warren Head. But this would be the beginning for many of the men who would find it very hard to adapt back into civilian life. I believe the building in the background is No. 52 Bargates, which would place the photograph not far from the British Legion Club at 61-63 Bargates. To the left of the telegraph pole can be seen the Baptist church on the corner of Beaconsfield Road.

The Royal British Legion was formed on 15 May 1921. It brought together four national organisations of ex-servicemen that had established themselves after the First World War. Over 6 million people served in the conflict, 725,000 of whom never returned. Of those that did, 1.75 million had some form of permanent disability. Christchurch itself lost many men during both world wars and, closer to my own generation, in the Falklands and in Bosnia. The full list of the fallen can be found within the Priory.

A VIEW DOWN Bargates, looking towards the railway bridge, in March 2012. Much has changed since 1919, and many of the original buildings have been demolished and replaced with modern buildings. Beaconsfield Road can just be seen on the right of the picture and the Baptist church is just out of shot.

79

THE CONGREGATIONAL CHURCH (NOW ELIM PENTECOSTAL CHURCH)

THIS PHOTOGRAPH SHOWS a boys' day trip in the 1920s. I wonder where they were headed? Teachers and parents are on hand to look after them. In the background can just be seen the

United Reformed church, formerly the Congregational church on Millhams Street, just off the main Christchurch High Street. The church was built in and around 1866 and designed by W. Stint of Westminster. Attached to the church were two schools, a boys' school and a girls' school.

ELIM PENTECOSTAL CHURCH, formerly the United Reformed church, seen here in March 2012. The two schools have long gone, and the area has been redeveloped. You can now walk from Saxon Square down the alleyway and come out within Millhams Street, next to the church and across from the area which was once the site of the schools. In 1960 the church celebrated 300 years of worship within the town.

WICK FERRY
HOLIDAY CAMP

WICK FERRY HOLIDAY Camp in the 1950s. It was located at No. 43 Wick Lane. Notice that the accommodation is all beach hut-type villas: many of the holiday camps of the time used facilities like this. Wick Ferry Holiday Camp closed in the 1960s, only to be taken over by Pontins' holiday camp. This opened here in 1962, with 224 chalets. It was one of the first to be entirely

self-catering. The main entertainment building was designed to look like a miniature Festival Hall.

PONTINS SURVIVED UNTIL 1995, when it closed and was demolished. A new hotel, Captain's Club Hotel, was built on the site in 2002 and the surrounding area, where all of the chalets once stood, has been redeveloped and houses built on it. The modern picture shows the Wick Ferry, which has plied its trade across the river for over 250 years and in a certain way has relied on the passing trade and the hotels and holiday camps to survive.

HENGISTBURY HEAD

A POSTCARD VIEW of Hengistbury Head in the 1930s. The area has seen many changes of use through the years. Archaeological records suggest that Hengistbury Head was an ancient centre of metal working, using the local iron deposits. Then, during the seventeenth and eighteenth centuries, it became a place used by smugglers to land great cargoes of contraband, using the double dykes as a place to conceal both their wagons and their escape. There are stories of

students at the grammar school at the Lady Chapel of Christchurch Priory church seeing the smugglers, with armed guards out in front and behind, wending their way along the route to Wick to cross the River Stour en route to the New Forest.

AS YOU CAN see, the view has not changed much and instead of being frequented by smugglers, the area is a place where, in the summer months, holidaymakers flock, and either sit on the beach or go for a walk over Hengistbury Head and down to the sandy beach at Mudeford Spit. In 2011, Hengistbury Head saw the return of the Kite Festival to its true home.

CHRISTCHURCH HAVEN

CHRISTCHURCH HAVEN IN Mudeford in around 1907, showing the narrow harbour entrance and the famous Haven Inn run by Hannah Sellers and her husband. The whole of this area is made up of gravel and ironstone – a perfect landing place for smugglers, on which they could easily beach their vessels and then wait for high tide to float them off again. This is also the site, in 1784, of the famous Battle of Mudeford, where William Allen (revenue officer) was shot and killed. A smuggler by the name of George Coombes was caught, hanged and gibbeted for the murder.

THE CONSTRUCTION, IN the 1950s, of the Haven car park means that the original Haven Inn can no longer be seen. It has been replaced, but if you walk to the end of Mudeford Quay, standing behind the present Haven Inn, you will find a building with steps up the front. This is the original Haven Inn. Standing to the right of the picture can just be seen the lifeboat station. The age-old art of crabbing – seeing how many crabs you can catch by dangling a line into the harbour – is practiced here, and when I was a child I can remember, on a Sunday afternoon, being brought down to the Haven to catch a crab or two. If you walk down to the end of the Haven, towards Mudeford Quay, you will also be able to purchase some of the best fresh fish within the area.

CHRISTCHURCH HARBOUR

AN AERIAL VIEW of Christchurch Harbour in the 1930s. This picture shows the two rivers, the River Stour and the River Avon, meeting, and in the background you can just make out part of Christchurch Harbour. In days gone by, the sea was a vital link to the town. The records of Abram Pike (the local revenue officer) from 1802/03 show that at the quay, along with the Haven, ships would unload cargo such as coal from Portsmouth and Southampton, along with other commodities such as tea, vinegar, tallow, candles, butter and soap – all coming into the town via the sea.

Then there were three breweries at Christchurch (along with thirty pubs/inns), and there are records that showed vessels would come into the quay and load up with beer, which was then taken to Portsmouth. The harbour itself has been the centre of many a scheme, and altered many times over the years, but today it is a centre for pleasure crafts and leisure activities.

I WAS UNABLE to take the photograph from the same vantage point today, so these photographs have been taken from the top of the tower at the Priory. As you can see, the view is somewhat different: you can see how areas of the harbour and river frontage have changed.

Just picking out one area as an example, if you look down to where the Christchurch Yacht Club is you can see how the area has been turned into a large and expensive housing estate with boat moorings. Stretching out in front is Stanpit Marsh and the harbour, and you can also just make out in the background the Isle of Wight.

THE CAT AND FIDDLE

THE CAT AND FIDDLE on the Lyndhurst Road near Christchurch in 1933. It was once a coaching inn: they would have changed horses here en route to Holmsley station. Also, as with most of the local inns, it was frequented by many a smuggler from within the area. Maybe Isaac Gulliver, one of the most famous of the local smugglers, stopped off here for a drink or two?

Over the original door can also be found a woodcarving of the nursery rhyme from which the inn takes its name. This carving dates back over 300 years. The sign hanging outside is of the cat about to play a tune – 'Take this Cup of Sparkling Wine'.

THE INN HAS gone through many a change since 1933. Now it is a Harvester and it has been redecorated, removing much of its original character. The carving which had hung for hundreds of years over the front door was damaged during the last war. Next time you visit the inn, take time to see it, and also to see the sign showing the cat about to play a tune.

FRIARS ROAD, FRIARS CLIFF

VIEW DOWN FRIARS Road at Friars Cliff in the 1950s. To the left of the picture you can see an old P series Rover, which shows this was an affluent area.

WHAT A DIFFERENCE! Many of the trees have gone, and those that are left have matured. The old lampposts have been replaced by characterless versions. If you carry on walking down Friars Road you will in the end come to beautiful sandy Avon Beach. In the summer months, what with being so close to the beach, the area transforms into a bustling space with all of the visitors trying to find

somewhere to park, or just making their way down to the beach. Local road names such as Smugglers Lane also hint at previous occupations in this area.

SOPLEY CHURCH

SOPLEY CHURCH, ON the road from Christchurch to Ringwood, at the turn of the twentieth century. The church of St Michael and All Angels was built in the twelfth century on a mound overlooking the River Avon and the mill on a site that may well have housed a Saxon church. The church served the local manor, which predates the Norman Conquest. This area supported the Royalist faction during the Civil War and a Thomas Lake, who was incumbent here, allowed the congregation to celebrate when the King was victorious. In front of the church is the mill, mentioned in the Domesday Book. A sum of 10s was paid annually, as well as 875 eels. The mill that now stands in front of the church is not the original one: it was built in 1878. The mill wheels were turned via an undershot wheel (i.e. the water fed the bottom of the wheel, rather than the top). However, this was later changed to a turbine. The mill operated up to 1946.

LYING JUST OFF the main road between Ringwood and Christchurch, you cannot today miss the church. As you approach the one-way system around the Woolpack Inn, turn left (up the country lane), drive to the end of the lane and you will find the church standing on a mound in front of the mill and the River Avon. Running past the village is a small stream which makes its way through the village past the Woolpack Inn before it joins up with the River Avon.

If you enjoyed this book, you may also be interested in…

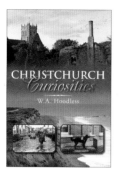

Christchurch Curiosities
W.A. HOODLESS

A quirky compendium of little-known stories and facts about the beautiful heritage town of Christchurch. From an amazing tale about some Royalty Fishery salmon, to the story of how the prior persuaded King Henry VIII to exempt the Priory Church from the Dissolution, and the strange phenomenon of the River Avon 'freezing the wrong way round', it is full of accounts that will delight and entertain: both residents and visitors will find much to marvel at here.

978 0 7524 5670 6

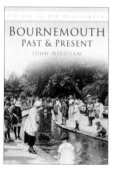

Bournemouth Past & Present
JOHN NEEDHAM

Bournemouth Past & Present charts the town's history through a variety of images depicting scenes of yesteryear contrasted with images of contemporary views. The archive images show the gardens where the balloon now stands freshly laid out with a large fountain, and streets busy with trams and carts. Accompanied by informative captions, this volume will rekindle fond memories in the older members of the town, and reveal a different Bournemouth for younger members.

978 0 7524 5569 3

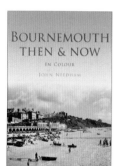

Bournemouth Then & Now
JOHN NEEDHAM

This fascinating book explores the transformations that have seen Bournemouth develop from a small seaside town into a major South Coast resort and bustling centre of commerce. Archive images are contrasted with modern photographs taken from the same vantage point and show how Bournemouth has changed – as well as the familiar landmarks that have remained. *Bournemouth Then & Now* will delight residents and visitors alike.

978 0 7524 6792 4

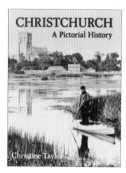

Christchurch: A Pictoral History
CHRISTINE TAYLOR

Christchurch is surrounded by large wide marshes at the confluence of the Stour and the Avon. Its harbour was sheltered by nearby Hengistbury Head, a defensible site in more turbulent days, as well as an excellent look-out point. Its skyline is dominated by the Priory, which was famous in the Middle Ages for its relics and attracted many pilgrims. After the Reformation and, a century later, the Civil War, Christchurch fell into decline and became a small fishing town.

978 0 8503 3901 7

Visit our website and discover thousands of other History Press books.
www.thehistorypress.co.uk

The History Press